Is rain fun?

Sam and Dan go to the pond. Sam has fishing rods and a mat to sit on.

2

Dan has a bucket of bait.

3

Just as they get the rods
set up, it rains.

Dan and Sam sit on the log
and wait for the rain to stop.

They spot a big fish. It jumps
out of the pond and plops
back in.

They spot a frog on a
rock. It has a big grin.

Then ten ducks flap into
the pond. They quack
and swim in a zigzag.

Snails sail off.
It is a trail of snails.

A fox runs to the pond.
He flicks the rain off his tail.

A fat rat pops up on to a log.
He lets the rain drip on him.

Dan and Sam drop the
mat and let the rain drip
and drop on them.

The rain will not stop the
fun. Dan and Sam splish
and splash in the rain.

Sam stands on the log.
He fills his hands up with rain.

14

Sam and Dan think
the rain is fun but
they are not fans of hail!

Words to blend

will	fish	lunch
six	fishing	bucket
such	rock	ducks
quack	swim	zigzag
off	fox	flicks
splish	splash	think

Before reading

Synopsis: Dan and Sam go fishing. It's raining but they see lots of happy creatures in the rain and start to enjoy themselves. Then it starts to hail!

Review phoneme/s: th ch ng sh

New phoneme: ai

Story discussion: Look at the cover, and read the title together. Ask: *What do you think? Can rain be fun? Does it look like fun in the picture? What might happen in this story?*

Link to prior learning: Display the grapheme *ai*. Say: *These two letters are a digraph. That means they make one sound together. They make the /ai/ sound, as in* rain. *This digraph can come at the start or in the middle of a word.* Turn to page 4 and challenge children to find and read three words with *ai* (rain, pain, rains).

Vocabulary check: Bait – scraps of fish food used in fishing to make the fish swallow the hook. Look at the word *bait* on page 3 and in the picture on page 2. Talk about how Sam and Dan will use the bait to help them catch fish. Can children see what the bait is? (maggots or worms)

Decoding practice: Give children a card with the digraph *ai*, and cards or magnetic letters l, t, b, r, n. Can they make the words *tail, bait* and *nail*? What other real words can they make? (e.g. bail, trail, rail, train, etc.) Encourage partners to read each other's words.

Tricky word practice: Display the word *into*. Ask children to draw a line to split it into two little words: in/to. Ask: *Which is the tricky part of this word?* (The *o*, which makes an /oo/ sound.) Make a list of other words with this spelling pattern and sound, e.g. do, to. Encourage children to practise writing and reading these words.

After reading

Apply learning: Talk about the end of the story. Ask: *Have you ever been outdoors in a hailstorm? What is hail like? Do you agree with Dan and Sam that it's not as much fun as the rain?*

Comprehension

- What special equipment did Sam and Dan take fishing with them?

- How many fish did they catch in the end?

- Can you remember all the different animals that Dan and Sam saw?

Fluency

- Pick a page that most of the group read quite easily. Ask them to reread it with pace and expression. Model how to do this if necessary.

- Turn to page 13. Can children read the words with expression and enthusiasm? Model how to read the onomatopoeic words *splish* and *splash* if necessary. Ask: *Can you hear how these words sound a bit like rain falling?*

- Practise reading the words on page 17.

Tricky words review

was	for	his
go	me	they
into	of	no
he	are	has
all	as	we